IT'S TIME TO EAT BEAN BURRITOS

It's Time to Eat BEAN BURRITOS

Walter the Educator

SKB
Silent King Books
A WhichHead Entertainment Imprint

Copyright © 2024 by Walter the Educator

All rights reserved. No part of this book may be reproduced in any manner whatsoever without written per- mission except in the case of brief quotations embodied in critical articles and reviews.

First Printing, 2024

Disclaimer

This book is a literary work; the story is not about specific persons, locations, situations, and/or circumstances unless mentioned in a historical context. Any resemblance to real persons, locations, situations, and/or circumstances is coincidental. This book is for entertainment and informational purposes only. The author and publisher offer this information without warranties expressed or implied. No matter the grounds, neither the author nor the publisher will be accountable for any losses, injuries, or other damages caused by the reader's use of this book. The use of this book acknowledges an understanding and acceptance of this disclaimer.

It's Time to Eat BEAN BURRITOS is a collectible early learning book by Walter the Educator suitable for all ages belonging to Walter the Educator's Time to Eat Book Series. Collect more books at WaltertheEducator.com

USE THE EXTRA SPACE TO TAKE NOTES AND DOCUMENT YOUR MEMORIES

BEAN BURRITOS

It's time to munch on something neat,

It's Time to Eat Bean Burritos

A bean burrito, warm and sweet!

Wrapped in a tortilla, soft and round,

With beans inside, it's flavor-bound.

Inside, it's cozy, filled with beans,

A tasty treat for kings and queens!

Brown and creamy, soft and warm,

A burrito hug in a tasty form.

Maybe a sprinkle of cheese on top,

Or rice that makes each flavor pop.

Some like it spicy, some like it mild,

Each little burrito makes us smile!

We take a bite, it's warm and nice,

Beans and flavors wrapped up tight.

With salsa drips or a sour cream dip,

Every bite is a tasty trip!

It's Time to Eat

Bean Burritos

For lunch or snack or dinner, too,

A bean burrito's fun to chew.

Folded up tight, no mess or fuss,

It's a perfect treat for all of us!

Soft on the outside, cozy within,

Every bite brings a big grin.

Beans are healthy, full of fun,

In each burrito for everyone!

Sometimes with corn or veggies green,

Every burrito is a tasty scene.

Wrapped up snug, so round and neat,

A bean burrito is such a treat!

With every munch, the flavors grow,

Beans and rice put on a show.

It's Time to Eat

Bean Burritos

From the first bite to the very last,

Bean burritos are a tasty blast!

So let's gather round, it's time to eat,

Bean burritos can't be beat!

Warm and soft, they bring delight

A yummy snack that feels just right.

Folded and wrapped, with beans inside,

Bean burritos make us smile wide.

A tasty meal, so snug and sweet

It's Time to Eat

Bean Burritos

Bean burritos are the best to eat!

ABOUT THE CREATOR

Walter the Educator is one of the pseudonyms for Walter Anderson. Formally educated in Chemistry, Business, and Education, he is an educator, an author, a diverse entrepreneur, and he is the son of a disabled war veteran. "Walter the Educator" shares his time between educating and creating. He holds interests and owns several creative projects that entertain, enlighten, enhance, and educate, hoping to inspire and motivate you. Follow, find new works, and stay up to date with Walter the Educator™

at WaltertheEducator.com